Burning
CARBON

What is energy?

Energy makes my iPad work.

It makes my torch work.

Energy makes the car go.

It makes my dad's **wheelchair** go.

Burning carbon

We can **burn** carbon
to make energy.
Look at the fire.
We can burn carbon
in the fire.

We burn carbon here.

Smoke

Look at the **smoke**.

The carbon will burn and make the smoke.

We can see the smoke.

Gas

The carbon will burn
and make gas.

We can not see the gas.

We can not smell the gas.

The gas is here.

The gas is here.

The gas is here too.